Love One Another As I Have Loved You

Prayers, Meditations and Reflections on Family Love

Gareth Byrne

VERITAS

Published 2016 by Veritas Publications
7–8 Lower Abbey Street
Dublin 1, Ireland
publications@veritas.ie
www.veritas.ie

ISBN 978 1 84730 760 6

10 9 8 7 6 5 4 3 2 1

Designed by Heather Costello, Veritas Publications
Printed in the Republic of Ireland by Walsh Colour Print, Co. Kerry

Veritas books are printed on paper made from the wood pulp of
managed forests. For every tree felled, at least one tree is planted,
thereby renewing natural resources.

Introduction: Reflecting on the Joy of Love

The publication by Pope Francis of *Amoris laetitia – The Joy of Love*, his apostolic exhortation 'on Love in the Family' (2016), following the two meetings of the Synod of Bishops on this theme in 2014 and 2015, prompts us to reflect prayerfully on life and love, the Christian vocation, marriage and family, friendship, community, and the hope that is within us as Christians. Jesus has shown us the depths of God's love and we seek to mirror that love by loving one another:

> This is my commandment, that you love one another as I have loved you. No one has greater love than this, to lay down one's life for one's friends. (John 15:12–13)

Pope Francis has indicated time and again his concern to support and empower families. He is convinced that, despite the ups and downs of family life, family, in one way or another, is central to the well-being and development of all human persons. When we take quiet time in the healing presence of Jesus, with his look of love upon us, we recognise, in ever new ways, who we are called to be. In his love, we acknowledge our strengths and weaknesses, our hopes and fears, our desires, needs and responsibilities, and look beyond ourselves to the other:

> We need to learn to pray over our past history, to accept ourselves, to learn how to live with our limitations, and even to forgive ourselves, in order to have this same attitude towards others. (*Amoris laetitia*, 107)

This book is designed to help us to pray in the context of family, near and far, supported by the whole community of our love and by our community of faith the Church, the family we form together around Christ. Pope Francis reminds us to open ourselves in love to others, no matter how they present themselves to us:

True love is always contemplative, and permits us to serve the other not out of necessity or vanity, but rather because he or she is beautiful beyond mere appearances. (*Evangelii Gaudium*, 199)

In this book you will find material for prayer and meditation. You will find relevant passages from Scripture and from the saints, from Vatican II, from *Share the Good News: National Directory for Catechesis in Ireland*, and in particular from the heart and hand of Pope Francis. In quiet moments with Jesus, in our parish church, at home, out walking, waiting for a friend, we can learn to count our blessings, ask for a deepening conversion of our own heart, pray for the response we yearn for from those whom we love, and send out our love to them, tenderly, wherever they may be.

Pope Francis, promising us his prayers and asking for ours, reminds us to be confident in each other, and in Christ, who invites us to the fullness of life, prayer and love:

> I pray that the Lord may continue to deepen your love for him, and that this love may manifest itself in your love for one another and for the Church. Pray often and take the fruits of your prayer into the world, that all may know Jesus Christ and his merciful love. Please pray also for me, for I truly need your prayers and will depend on them always!
> (Francis, Manila, Philippines, 2015)

Love is Patient, Love is Kind

In a lyrical passage from St Paul, we see some of the features of true love:

Love is patient,
love is kind;
love is not jealous or boastful;
it is not arrogant or rude.
Love does not insist on its own way,
it is not irritable or resentful;
it does not rejoice at wrong,
but rejoices in the right.
Love bears all things,
believes all things,
hopes all things,
endures all things. (1 COR 13:4–7)

Love is experienced and nurtured in the daily life of couples and their children.

FRANCIS, AMORIS LAETITIA, 90

Everything is related, and we human beings are united as brothers and sisters on a wonderful pilgrimage, woven together by the love God has for each of his creatures and which also unites us in fond affection with brother sun, sister moon, brother river and mother earth.

FRANCIS, LAUDATO SI', 92

We Should Not Be Afraid of Loving One Another

We should not be afraid of loving people and telling them that we love them. This is the greatest nourishment of all.

JEAN VANIER

Family Prayer

God be with our family,
from the youngest to the oldest
lighting up our relations,
sowing grace into our troubles.
God be with our family,
weaving love into our work,
our rest, our play.
Amen.

ANON

The Lord's presence dwells in real and concrete families, with all their daily troubles and struggles, joys and hopes … The spirituality of family love is made up of thousands of small but real gestures. In that variety of gifts and encounters which deepen communion, God has his dwelling place.

AMORIS LAETITIA, 315

How Lovely is Your Dwelling Place, Lord

How lovely is your dwelling place,
Lord, God of hosts.
My soul is longing and yearning,
is yearning for the courts of the Lord.
My heart and my soul ring out their joy
to God the living God.
The sparrow herself finds a home
and the swallow a nest for her brood;
she lays her young at your altars,
Lord of hosts, my king and my God.
They are happy who dwell in your house,
for ever singing your praise …
O, Lord God of hosts, hear my prayer,
give ear, O God of Jacob.
Turn your eyes, O God our shield,
look on the face of your anointed.
One day within your courts
is better than a thousand elsewhere …
Lord, God of hosts,
Happy the one who trusts in you!

PSALM 84

Love Coexists with Imperfection

Love does not have to be perfect for us to value it. The other person loves me as best they can, with all their limits, but the fact that love is imperfect does not mean that it is untrue or unreal. It is real, albeit limited and earthly. If I expect too much, the other person will let me know, for he or she can neither play God nor serve all my needs. Love coexists with imperfection. It 'bears all things' and can hold its peace before the limitations of the loved one.

Amoris laetitia, 113

If we accept that God's love is unconditional, that the Father's love cannot be bought or sold, then we will be capable of showing boundless love and forgiving others even if they have wronged us.

Amoris laetitia, 108

I thank God that many families, which are far from considering themselves perfect, live in love, fulfil their calling and keep moving forward, even if they fall many times along the way.

Amoris laetitia, 57

Fall in Love, Stay in Love

Nothing is more practical than finding God,
that is, than falling in love in a quite absolute way.

What you are in love with, what seizes your imagination
will affect everything.

It will decide what will get you out of bed in the mornings,
what you will do with your evenings,
how you will spend your weekends,
what you will read, who you know,
what breaks your heart,
and what amazes you with joy and gratitude.

Fall in love, stay in love,
and it will decide everything.

PEDRO ARRUPE

Ever the Maker and Keeper of My Days

O God, you search me and you know me.
All my ways lie open to your gaze.
When I walk or lie down, you go before me:
ever the maker and keeper of my days.

You know my resting and my rising.
You discern my purpose from afar,
and with love everlasting you besiege me:
God of my present, my past and future too.

Although your Spirit is upon me,
still I search for shelter from your light.
There is nowhere on earth I can escape you:
even the darkness is radiant in your sight.

For you created me and shaped me,
gave me life within my mother's womb.
For the wonder of who I am I praise you:
safe in your hands, all creation is made new.

PSALM 139, ARR. BERNADETTE FARRELL

The Life of the Christian

In reflecting on the life of the Christian alive with the fruit of the Spirit, nine facilitating conditions for spiritual growth have been identified and recommended:

A developing self-concept with accurate self-perception and loving self-acceptance;

A responsible awareness of one's needs, feelings and emotions;

A sense of autonomy or inner-directedness;

An appreciation of genuine authority;

A morality based on self-chosen but universally valid principles of love;

An orientation toward others as persons, not as objects;

A view of spiritual growth as intrinsically related to physical, emotional, and intellectual development;

A centredness on present times and places as avenues of God's activity;

An openness to the transcendent in the reality of self, others, and world.

DANIEL A. HELMINIAK

To Dream in the Family

It is important to dream in the family. All mothers and fathers dream of their sons and daughters in the womb for nine months. They dream of how they will be. It isn't possible to have a family without such dreams. When you lose this capacity to dream you lose the capacity to love, the capacity to love is lost. I recommend that at night when you examine your consciences, ask yourself if you dreamed of the future of your sons and daughters. Did you dream of your husband or wife? Did you dream today of your parents, your grandparents …

Just as the gift of the Holy Family was entrusted to Saint Joseph, so the gift of the family and its place in God's plan is entrusted to us so we can carry it forward.

Francis, Manila, 16 January 2015

Prayer to St Joseph

Saint Joseph,
gentle spouse and loving friend of Mary,
guardian of her son Jesus, the Son of God,
watch over and protect us,
the brothers and sisters, the neighbours and friends, of Jesus.
Keep us in your prayers whether we are awake or asleep.
Help us to hold our hearts ever open to God's plans for us,
to the surprises he keeps in store for us,
to the dreams we have of who we can be in God's kindness.
With Mary, encourage us to say 'yes' to God's invitation to love,
and to respond to him full of hope and peace.
May our family, our parish, the wider community, and all creation,
welcome Christ with you and sing for joy at the wonders of God's work. Amen.

Gareth Byrne

According to Your Word

Gabriel came to Mary and said, 'Greetings, favoured one!
The Lord is with you.'

LUKE 1:28

Hail Mary, full of grace,
The Lord is with you.
Blessed are you among women
And blessed is the fruit of your womb,
Jesus.

Then Mary said: 'Here am I, the servant of the Lord; let it
be done with me according to your word.'

LUKE 1:38

Holy Mary, mother of God,
Pray for us sinners, now
and at the hour of our death.
Amen.

Sé do Bheatha, a Mhuire

Sé do Bheatha, a Mhuire,
atá lán de ghrásta,
tá an Tiarna leat.
Is beannaithe thú idir mhná,
agus is beannaithe toradh do bhroinne, Íosa.
A Naomh Mhuire, a mháthair Dé,
guigh orainn, na peacaigh,
anois agus ar uair ár mbáis.
Áiméan.

Here Are My Brother and Sister and Mother

And pointing to his disciples, Jesus said, 'Here are my mother and my brothers! For whoever does the will of my Father in heaven is my brother and sister and mother.'

MATTHEW 12:49–50

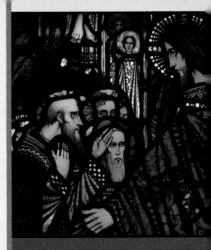

No one is without a family in this world: the Church is a home and family for everyone, especially those who 'labour and are heavy burdened' (Mt 11:28).

ST JOHN PAUL II, *FAMILIARIS CONSORTIO*, 85

'Come to me, all you that are weary and are carrying heavy burdens, and I will give you rest. Take my yoke upon you, and learn from me; for I am gentle and humble in heart, and you will find rest for your souls. For my yoke is easy and my burden is light.'

MATTHEW 11:28–9

God calls us to become, together, one family, working in common purpose, in communion with God and with one another.

SHARE THE GOOD NEWS, 26

The Family of the Church

God and Father of us all,
in Jesus, your Son and our Saviour,
you have made us
your sons and daughters
in the family of the Church.
May your grace and love
help our families
in every part of the world
be united to one another
in fidelity to the Gospel.
May the example of the Holy Family,
with the aid of your Holy Spirit,
guide all families, especially those most troubled,
to be homes of communion and prayer
and to always seek your truth and live in your love.
Through Christ our Lord. Amen.
Jesus, Mary and Joseph, pray for us!

WORLD MEETING OF FAMILIES PRAYER, PHILADELPHIA 2015

Our Loved Ones Merit Our Complete Attention

It is a profound spiritual experience to contemplate our loved ones with the eyes of God and to see Christ in them. This demands a freedom and openness which enables us to appreciate their dignity. We can be fully present to others only by giving fully of ourselves and forgetting all else. Our loved ones merit our complete attention. Jesus is our model in this, for whenever people approached to speak with him, he would meet their gaze, directly and lovingly (cf. Mk 10:21).

Amoris laetitia, 323

Jesus looking at him, loved him. (Mark 10:21)
Jesus said to her, 'I am he', the one who is speaking to you. (John 4:26)
Jesus took him by the hand and lifted him up, and he was able to stand. (Mark 9:27)
'Were not our hearts burning within us while he was talking to us and while he was opening the Scriptures to us?' (Luke 24:32)

To today's young people I say: be more docile to the voice of the Spirit, let the great expectations of the Church, of mankind, resound in the depths of your hearts. Do not be afraid to open your minds to Christ the Lord who is calling. Feel his loving look upon you and respond enthusiastically to Jesus when he asks you to follow him without reserve.

St John Paul II, *Pastores dabo vobis*, 82

Take Time, Quality Time

Dialogue is essential for experiencing, expressing and fostering love in marriage and family life. Yet it can only be the fruit of a long and demanding apprenticeship. Men and women, young people and adults, communicate differently. They speak different languages and they act in different ways. Our way of asking and responding to questions, the tone we use, our timing and any number of other factors, condition how well we communicate.

Take time, quality time. This means being ready to listen patiently and attentively to everything the other person wants to say ... Do not be rushed, put aside all your own needs and worries, and make space. Often the other spouse does not need a solution to his or her problems, but simply to be heard, to feel that someone has acknowledged their pain, their disappointment, their fear, their anger, their hopes and their dreams.

All family life is a 'shepherding' in mercy. Each of us, by our love and care, leaves a mark on the life of others.

AMORIS LAETITIA, 136, 137, 322

At the Service of Communion

In a sense, all the sacraments have a healing effect and are at the service of communion. Holy Orders and Marriage do, however, confer a particular mission in the Church and serve to build up the 'People of God' through the service of others.

SHARE THE GOOD NEWS, 56

To be a priest today takes the heart of a hermit, the soul of a mountain climber, the eyes of a lover, the hands of a healer, the compassion of one who sees the whole world as part of himself. It requires total immersion in the life of Christ.

DANIEL O'LEARY

Prayer for Vocations

O God, our Father, you have called us in Baptism to follow your Son, Jesus Christ, through lives of loving service to you and to one another. Grant us your assistance as we seek to live out our vocation in life.

We pray especially for those who have answered your call as priests, brothers, sisters, deacons, and lay ministers. Keep them faithful in following your Son and dedicated in serving their brothers and sisters.

Grant that many more men and women will be open to the challenge of dedicating their lives in the ministry of building your Kingdom.

UNITED STATES BISHOPS' CONFERENCE

Commitment to Love and Life

In the Bible, there is no stronger image of the covenant between God and God's people than married love. The mutual love of man and woman is an image of the absolute and unfailing love with which God loves us. In the sacrament of marriage, the promise made by a man and a woman to be faithful to each other, all their days, and their openness to the children they may receive, establishes between them a partnership of the whole of life, 'an unbreakable union of their two lives'. Christian marriage reflects the New Covenant between Christ and the Church, the Bride for whom he gives his life. As a commitment to love and life, Christian marriage, blessed by God, builds up the ecclesial community and is deserving of its full support. Christian marriage is a true sacrament, signifying and communicating grace, echoing the faithful love of God.

Share the Good News, 56

Married love is an eminently human love because it is an affection between two persons rooted in the will and it embraces the good of the whole person; it can enrich the sentiments of the spirit and their physical expression with a unique dignity and ennoble them as the special features and manifestations of the friendship proper to marriage … A love like that, bringing together the human and the divine, leads the partners to a free and mutual self-giving, experienced in tenderness and action, and permeating their whole lives.

Vatican II, *Gaudium et spes*, 49

Set Me as a Seal upon Your Heart

Set me as a seal upon your heart
as a seal upon your arm;
for love is strong as death,
passion fierce as the grave.
Its flashes are flashes of fire,
a raging flame.
Many waters cannot quench love,
neither can floods drown it.

SONG OF SOLOMON 8:6–7A

Lightness

It was your lightness that drew me,
the lightness of your talk and your laughter,
the lightness of your cheek in my hands,
your sweet gentle modest lightness;
and it is the lightness of your kiss
that is starving my mouth,
and the lightness of your embrace
that will let me go adrift.

MEG BATEMAN, TRANSLATED FROM THE
GAELIC BY THE AUTHOR

Respect Is the Heart of Love

A friendship can exist only by letting the other person be other, and by virtue of the mystery which the other person will always remain. The more intimately two people love, the more they confirm their being different. To know a person well on this level means to acknowledge and to accept the fact that there is always more to be known; one never exhausts the potential of the beloved ... Only a deep respect for the continuance of this mystery can create the atmosphere in which marriage or friendship or community can grow and blossom. Respect is the heart of love just as lack of respect is its end.

PETER G. VAN BREEMEN

Some people today choose to remain single. They see this vocation as the most appropriate for them, taking up the opportunity to dedicate themselves in a variety of ways to the service of others. There are many too who may feel they did not choose a single life, but who have learned to live that vocation actively and positively. Some have found themselves single parents. Others having followed a call to marriage, have for a variety of reasons come to live the single life again. Among those who have been married but have separated, some take on the responsibility of caring for their children, for the most part alone. Many of course by God's providence, find themselves, at a particular point in their life, widows or widowers, and perhaps having raised a family, living a newfound vocation to the single life.

Like everyone, single people need support in the Christian life ... Their particular faith journey needs to be sustained within the faith community, and opportunities provided for enrichment and growth ... Having met Jesus and his Church, no one should ever feel alone.

SHARE THE GOOD NEWS, 85

Faithful Friends

Faithful friends are a sturdy shelter:
whoever finds one has found a treasure.
Faithful friends are beyond price;
no amount can balance their worth.
Faithful friends are life-saving medicine;
and those who fear the Lord will find
them.

SIRACH 6:14–16

A friend who can be silent with us
in a moment of despair or confusion,
who can stay with us in an hour
of grief and bereavement,
who can tolerate not knowing …
not healing, not curing …
that is a friend who cares.

HENRI NOUWEN

Would you like to see God glorified
by you? Then rejoice in your brother's
progress and you will immediately give
glory to God.

ST JOHN CHRYSOSTOM (C.347–407)

They Help and Serve Each Other

Marital joy can be experienced even amid sorrow; it involves accepting that marriage is an inevitable mixture of enjoyment and struggles, tensions and repose, pain and relief, satisfactions and longings, annoyances and pleasures, but always on the path of friendship, which inspires married couples to care for one another: 'they help and serve each other'.

Amoris laetitia, 126

Love trusts, it sets free, it does not try to control, possess or dominate everything. This freedom, which fosters independence, an openness to the world around us and to new experiences, can only enrich and expand relationships. The spouses then share with one another the joy of all they have received and learned outside the family circle. At the same time, this freedom makes for sincerity and transparency, for those who know that they are trusted and appreciated can be open and hide nothing.

Amoris laetitia, 115

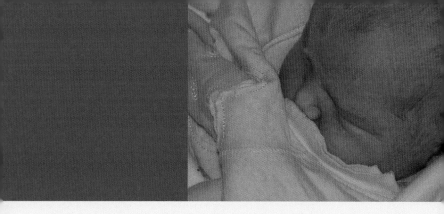

New Life, Welcomed as a Gift from God

The family is the setting in which a new life is not only born but also welcomed as a gift from God. Each new life 'allows us to appreciate the utterly gratuitous dimension of love, which never ceases to amaze us. It is the beauty of being loved first: children are loved even before they arrive'. Here we see the reflection of the primacy of the love of God, who always takes the initiative, for children 'are loved before having done anything to deserve it' …

The gift of a new child, entrusted by the Lord to a father and a mother, begins with acceptance, continues with lifelong protection and has as its final goal the joy of life eternal. By serenely contemplating the ultimate fulfilment of each human person, parents will be even more aware of the precious gift entrusted to them. For God allows parents to choose the name by which he himself will call their child for all eternity.

Amoris laetitia, 166

Christ has no body now, but yours.
No hands, no feet on earth but yours.
Yours are the eyes through which
Christ looks compassion on the world.
Yours are the feet
with which Christ walks to do good.
Yours are the hands
with which Christ blesses the world.

St Teresa of Avila (1515–82)

Honour Your Father and Mother

Honour your father and mother, that your days may be long in the land which the Lord your God is giving you.

Exodus 20:12; cf. Deuteronomy 5:16

Remember that it was of your parents you were born; how can you repay what they have given to you?

Sirach 7:28

Respect toward parents fills the home with light and warmth.

Catechism of the Catholic Church, 2219

Let all be convinced that human life and its transmission are realities whose meaning is not limited by the horizons of this life only: their true evaluation and full meaning can only be understood in reference to our eternal destiny.

Vatican II, Gaudium et spes, 51

The First School of Human Values

The family is the first school of human values, where we learn the wise use of freedom.

One of the things children need to learn from their parents is not to get carried away by anger.

Children need symbols, actions, stories ... Parents desirous of nurturing the faith of their children are sensitive to their patterns of growth, for they know that spiritual experience is not imposed but proposed. It is essential that children actually see that, for their parents, prayer is something truly important.

Amoris laetitia, 274, 269, 288

Education in the faith by the parents should begin in the child's earliest years. This already happens when family members help one another to grow in faith by the witness of a Christian life in keeping with the Gospel. Family catechesis precedes, accompanies and enriches other forms of instruction in the faith. Parents have the mission of teaching their children to pray and to discover their vocation as children of God.

Catechism of the Catholic Church, 2226

Lord,
Wrap your arms around my family,
and draw us close to you.
Amen.

Anon

Education into Freedom

Education includes encouraging the responsible use of freedom to face issues with good sense and intelligence. It involves forming persons who readily understand that their own lives, and the life of the community, are in their hands, and that freedom is itself a great gift.

Parents rely on schools to ensure the basic instruction of their children, but can never completely delegate the moral formation of their children to others. A person's affective and ethical development is ultimately grounded in a particular experience, namely, that his or her parents can be trusted. This means that parents, as educators, are responsible, by their affection and example, for instilling in their children trust and loving respect.

Parents are also responsible for shaping the will of their children, fostering good habits and a natural inclination to goodness. This entails presenting certain ways of thinking and acting as desirable and worthwhile, as part of a gradual process of growth. The desire to fit into society, or the habit of foregoing an immediate pleasure for the sake of a better and more orderly life in common, is itself a value that can inspire openness to greater values.

Amoris laetitia, 262, 263, 264

Godparents: Cultivating Faith

It is a very ancient custom of the Church that adults are not permitted to baptism without godparents, members of the Christian community who will assist the candidates at least in the final preparation for baptism and after baptism will help them persevere in the faith and in their lives as Christians. In the baptism of children, as well, godparents are to be present in order to represent both the expanded spiritual family of the one to be baptised and the role of Church as a mother. As occasion offers, godparents help the parents so that children will come to profess the faith and live up to it.

Rite of Christian Initiation of Adults, 8

Spiritual intelligence is inspired thought. It is light, the kiss of life that awakens our sleeping beauty. It animates people of any age, in any situation. In children, that quickening makes boys and girls want to seek out and cultivate their inborn gifts, energies, and desires ... let's stay open to that kiss of life. Let's trust in its existence ... The young can show us how to express our own spiritual truths.

Marsha Sinetar

I've found that there is always some beauty in life – in nature, sunshine, freedom, in yourself; these can help you. Look at these things, then you find yourself again, and God, and then you regain your balance.

Anne Frank

Children's Letters to God

Dear God,
I don't ever feel alone since I found out
about you.
Nora

Dear God,
I bet it is very hard for you to love all of
everybody in the whole world.
There are only 4 people in our family
and I can never do it.
Nan

Dear God,
I think about you sometimes even when
I am not praying.
Elliot

Dear God,
I am doing the best I can.
Frank

STUART HAMPLE AND ERIC
MARSHALL

The Elderly and the Young

Whenever we attempt to read the signs of the times it is helpful to listen to young people and the elderly. Both represent a source of hope for every people. The elderly bring with them memory and the wisdom of experience, which warns us not to foolishly repeat our past mistakes. Young people call us to renewed and expansive hope, for they represent new directions for humanity and open up the future, lest we cling to nostalgia for structures and customs which are no longer life-giving in today's world.

EVANGELII GAUDIUM, 108

Prayer to Saint Ann

O good Saint Ann,
mother of Mary, grandmother of Jesus,
intercede before God for our families
and their children.
May one generation hand on to another
faith in God's promise and
trust that he will do great things
for those who reverence his name.
Amen.

VICTOR HOAGLAND

Grandchildren are the crown
of the aged.
PROVERBS 17:6a

Prayer for Grandparents

Lord Jesus, you were born of the Virgin Mary,
the daughter of Saints Joachim and Anne.
Look with love on grandparents the world over.
Protect them! They are a source of enrichment
for families, for the Church and for all of society.
Support them! As they grow older,
may they continue to be for their families
strong pillars of Gospel faith,
guardians of noble domestic ideals,
living treasuries of sound religious traditions.
Make them teachers of wisdom and courage,
that they may pass on to future generations the fruits
of their mature human and spiritual experience.
Lord Jesus, help families and society
to value the presence and roles of grandparents.
May they never be ignored or excluded,
but always encounter respect and love.
Help them to live serenely and to feel welcomed
in all the years of life you have given them.
Mary, Mother of all the living,
keep grandparents constantly in your care,
accompany them on their earthly pilgrimage,
and, by your prayers, grant that all families
may one day be reunited in our heavenly homeland,
where you await all humanity
for the embrace of life without end.
Amen.

BENEDICT XVI

31

Who is My Neighbour?

Jesus knows the anxieties and tensions experienced by families and he weaves them into his parables: children who leave home to seek adventure (cf. Luke 15:11–32), or who prove troublesome (Matthew 21:28–31) or fall prey to violence (Mark 12:19).

AMORIS LAETITIA, 21

Wanting to justify himself, the lawyer asked Jesus 'And who is my neighbour?' Jesus replied, 'A man was going down from Jerusalem to Jericho, and fell into the hands of robbers, who stripped him, beat him, and went away, leaving him half dead. Now by chance a priest was going down the road; and when he saw him, he passed by on the other side. So likewise a Levite, when he came to the place and saw him, passed by on the other side. But a Samaritan while travelling came near him; and when he saw him, he was moved with pity. He went to him and bandaged his wounds, having poured oil and wine on them. Then he put him on his own animal, brought him to an inn, and took care of him. The next day he took out two denarii, gave them to the innkeeper, and said 'Take care of him; and when I come back, I will repay you whatever more you spend.' Which of the three, do you think, was a neighbour to the man who fell into the hands of the robbers? He said, 'The one who showed him mercy.' Jesus said to him, 'Go and do likewise.'

LUKE 10:29–37

The Gift of Self to Others

Christ proposes as the distinctive sign of his disciples the law of love and the gift of self to others (cf. Mt 22:39; Jn 13:34). He did so in stating a principle that fathers and mothers tend to embody in their own lives: 'No one has greater love than this, to lay down one's life for one's friends' (cf. Jn 8:1–11).

Amoris laetitia, 27

The duty of making oneself a neighbour to others and actively serving them becomes even more urgent when it involves the disadvantaged, in whatever area this may be. 'As you did it to one of the least of these my brethren, you did it to me.' (Mt 25:40).

Catechism of the Catholic Church, 1932

Lord,
Open our eyes
to the needs of our brothers and sisters;
inspire in us words and actions
to comfort those who labour and are burdened.
Make us serve them truly,
after the example of Christ and at his command.
And may your Church stand as a living witness
to truth and freedom,
to peace and justice,
that all people may be raised up to a new hope.

Eucharistic Prayer for Use in Masses for Various Needs IV

Christ Comes Disguised as a Stranger

I saw a stranger yesterday
I put food for him in the eating place,
drink for him in the drinking place,
music for him in the listening place;

And in the Holy Name of the Trinity,
he blessed myself and my house,
my possessions and my family.

And the lark said as she sang:
It is often, often, often,
Christ comes disguised as a stranger.

CELTIC RUNE OF HOSPITALITY

Do not neglect to show hospitality to
strangers, for by doing that some have
entertained angels without knowing it.

HEBREWS 13:2

Music Happens Inside You

Music happens inside you. It moves the
things that are there from place to place.
It can make them fly. It can bring you the
past. It can bring you things you did not
know. It can bring you into the moment
that is happening. It can bring you a cure.

TIMOTHY O'GRADY AND STEVE PYKE

Everyone Sang

Everyone suddenly burst out singing;
and I was filled with such delight
as prisoned birds must find in freedom,
winging wildly across the white
orchards and dark-green fields; on – on –
and out of sight.

Everyone's voice was suddenly lifted;
and beauty came like the setting sun:
My heart was shaken with tears; and horror
drifted away … O, but Everyone
was a bird; and the song was wordless; the
singing will never be done.

SIEGFRIED SASSOON

Each Moment Is a Gift

Christian spirituality proposes an alternative understanding of the quality of life, and encourages a prophetic and contemplative lifestyle …

We are speaking of an attitude of heart, one which approaches life with serene attentiveness, which is capable of being fully present to someone without thinking of what comes next, which accepts each moment as a gift from God to be lived to the full. Jesus taught us this attitude when he invited us to contemplate the lilies of the field and the birds of the air, or when seeing the rich young man and knowing his restlessness, 'he looked at him with love' (Mt 10:21) …

One expression of this attitude is when we stop and give thanks to God before and after meals. I ask all believers to return to this beautiful and meaningful custom. That moment of blessing, however brief, reminds us of our dependence on God for life; it strengthens our feeling of gratitude for the gifts of creation; it acknowledges those who by their labours provide us with these goods; and it reaffirms our solidarity with those in greatest need.

Laudato Si', 222, 226, 227

Almighty God,
Who filled the heart of Saint Columba
With the joy of the Holy Spirit
And with deep love for those in his care;
Grant by his intercession,
That your pilgrim people may follow him,
Strong in faith, sustained by hope,
And one in the love that binds us to you.
We ask this through Jesus Christ, our Lord.
Amen.

Roman Missal

Yours for Time and Eternity

My God I am yours for time
and eternity.
Lord I am yours forever.
It is you who must teach me
to trust in your Providence,
Loving Lord.

You are a God of love and
tenderness,
I place my trust in you.
And I ask that you grant me
acceptance of your will,
Loving Lord.

Take from my heart all painful
anxiety.
Let nothing sadden me but sin,
and then let my delight be,
hoping to see your face,
God, my all.

Suscipe of Venerable
Catherine McAuley (1778–
1841), arr. Elaine Deasy

Haiku on the Way

The still point of all
around which everything moves
is the love of God

Equal before God
every human being   all by
divine grace redeemed

When the heart of Christ
finds a home on Earth   someone
is blessing the world

DERMOT O'BRIEN

Lord God, we pray that you may be a
light in the darkness of our world.
We ask you that in the light you share
with us,
we become aware of the needs of your
people:
See the faces marred by frustration;
feel the thirst for justice;
be burned by the desire to be people
who care for each other.
Be with us we pray,
encouragement in our efforts,
and a sign of hope in Jesus your Son,
who is Lord forever and forever.
Amen.

DONAL NEARY

Clothe Yourself in Love

As God's chosen ones, holy and beloved, clothe yourselves in compassion, kindness, humility, meekness, and patience. Bear with one another and, if anyone has a complaint against another, forgive each other; just as the Lord has forgiven you, so you also must forgive. Above all, clothe yourselves with love, which binds everything together in perfect harmony. And let the peace of Christ rule in your hearts, to which indeed you were called in the one body. And be thankful. Let the word of Christ dwell in you richly; teach and admonish one another in all wisdom; and with gratitude in your hearts sing psalms, hymns, and spiritual songs to God. And whatever you do, in word or deed, do everything in the name of the Lord Jesus, giving thanks to God the Father through him.

COLOSSIANS 3:12–17

O Christ, our Morning Star, Splendour of Light Eternal, shining with the glory of the rainbow, come and waken us from the greyness of apathy and renew in us your gift of hope.

THE VENERABLE BEDE (673–735)

Sunday, the Day which Heals Us

The centurion answered, 'Lord, I am not worthy to have you come under my roof; only speak the word, and my servant will be healed.'

MATTHEW 8:8

In the Eucharist, fullness is already achieved; it is the living centre of the universe, the overflowing core of love and inexhaustible life. Joined to the incarnate Son, present in the Eucharist, the whole cosmos gives thanks to God. Indeed the Eucharist is itself an act of cosmic love ... the Eucharist joins heaven and earth; it embraces and penetrates all creation. The world that has come forth from God's hands returns to him in blessed and undivided adoration ...

On Sunday, our participation in the Eucharist has special importance. Sunday, like the Jewish Sabbath, is meant to be a day which heals our relationships with God, with ourselves, with others and with the world. Sunday is the day of Resurrection, the 'first day' of the new creation, whose first fruits are the Lord's risen humanity, the pledge of the final transfiguration of all created reality. It also proclaims 'man's eternal rest in God'. In this way Christian spirituality incorporates the values of relaxation and festivity.

LAUDATO SI', 236–7

Help Us to Spread Your Fragrance

Dear Jesus, help us to spread your fragrance
everywhere we go.
Flood our souls with your spirit and life.
Penetrate and possess our whole being so utterly,
that our lives may only be a radiance of yours.
Shine through us and be so in us,
that every soul we come in contact with
may feel your presence in our soul.
Let them look up and see no longer us, but only Jesus.
Stay with us and then we shall begin to shine as you shine,
so to shine as to be light to others.
The light, O Jesus, will be all from you.
None of it will be ours.
It will be you shining on others through us.
Let us thus praise you in the way you love best
by shining on those around us.
Let us preach you without preaching,
not by words, but by our example;
by the catching force –
the sympathetic influence of what we do,
the evident fullness of the love our hearts bear for you.
Amen.

ST TERESA OF KOLKATA/CALCUTTA

41

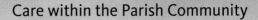

Care within the Parish Community

There is huge potential for parishes to do a lot more to acknowledge and to affirm the care that goes on within the faith community.

Affirmation does a number of things. For starters, it is always encouraging for people when what they do is noticed. In terms of faith, it helps people see God in what they are doing. It makes a connection between ordinary everyday life and church. It helps people see that religion is not a separate compartment of life. It testifies that religion is about how life is lived and how we care for one another.

Affirmation deepens discipleship.

DONAL HARRINGTON

The Church must accompany with attention and care the weakest of her children, who show signs of a wounded and troubled love, by restoring in them hope and confidence, like the beacon of a lighthouse in a port or a torch carried among the people to enlighten those who have lost their way or who are in the midst of a storm.

RELATIO SYNODI, 2014, 28

In the Midst of Human Weakness

I sincerely believe that Jesus wants a Church attentive to the goodness which the Holy Spirit sows in the midst of human weakness, a Mother who, while clearly expressing her objective teaching, 'always does what good she can, even if in the process, her shoes get soiled by the mud of the street'.

I encourage the faithful who find themselves in complicated situations to speak confidently with their pastors or with other lay people whose lives are committed to the Lord. They may not always encounter in them a confirmation of their own ideas or desires, but they will surely receive some light to help them better understand their situation and discover a path to personal growth.

Jesus himself is the shepherd of the hundred, not just of the ninety-nine.

Amoris laetitia, 308, 312, 309

43

Doing Little Things with Love

A spirituality that emerges from the experience of disability, and of life with disabled persons, gives great attention to human need, affectivity, suffering, hope and celebration. It invites the smart and self-reliant to a recognition of one's own finitude, fragility, and dependence upon others and God, because all human beings are disabled in one way or another, i.e. unable to meet the deepest aspirations and needs of the human heart by reliance on one's own strengths and resources. This is a spirituality that gives attention to the preciousness of human life, which is all the more so because it is so fragile … It is motivated by the conviction that the fullness of Christian life does not rest in doing great things, even under the pretext that they are for God's greater glory, but in doing little seemingly insignificant things with love.

MICHAEL DOWNEY

Who is like the wise man?
And who knows the interpretation
of a thing?
Wisdom makes one's face shine,
and the hardness of one's
countenance is changed.

ECCLESIASTES 8:1

The Lord bless you
and keep you;
The Lord make his face to shine
upon you,
and be gracious to you;
The Lord lift up his countenance upon you,
and give you his peace.

NUMBERS 6:24–6

A Community's Hidden Treasure

Old age is the most precious time of life, the one nearest eternity. There are two ways of growing old. There are old people who are anxious and bitter, living in the past and illusion, who criticise everything that goes on around them ... But there are also old people with a child's heart, who have used their freedom from function and responsibility to find a new youth. They have the wonder of a child, but the wisdom of maturity as well. They have integrated their years of function and so can live without being attached to power. Their freedom of heart and their acceptance of their limitations and weakness makes them people whose radiance illuminates the whole community. They are gentle and merciful, symbols of compassion and forgiveness. They become a community's hidden treasure, sources of unity and life.

JEAN VANIER

Old is cool because silver heads are no longer symbolic of an irrelevant past ... silver hair signifies an admirable ability to have weathered the storms of life. Those best able to vouch for the reliability of the holy and the sacred are those who have lived a life full of ups and downs. Those in their third age, who affirm life in all its fullness, are a priceless resource in communicating the viability and sustainability of an encounter with the holy.

PHILIP NORTH AND JOHN NORTH

The Power of Now

The power of now. That is the title of a bestseller in oriental-style spirituality. It points to a core truth for anyone who tries to pray. Freedom comes when I stop remembering the past or imagining the future. So much of life is preparation (work, meals, meetings …). To relax into the present is a relief. It becomes a space of restful recognising. It is where healing happens beyond the usual driven life.

MICHAEL PAUL GALLAGHER

We know that all things work together for good for those who love God.

ROMANS 8:28A

O what a beautiful story! What a beautiful book the Holy Spirit is now writing! It is in the press, not a day passes when the type is not being set, the ink not applied, the pages not being printed.

JEAN-PIERRE DE CAUSSADE
(1675–1751)

Love Always Has an Aspect of Deep Compassion

Patience takes root when I recognise that other people also have a right to live in the world, just as they are. It does not matter if they hold me back, if they unsettle my plans, or annoy me by the way they act or think, or if they are not everything I want them to be. Love always has an aspect of deep compassion that leads to accepting the other person as part of this world, even when he or she acts differently than I would like.

AMORIS LAETITIA, 92

Although the challenges may seem overwhelming, if we keep always before us the challenge to be protectors of the dignity of all members of the human family, we can bring the hope and light of faith to places of despair and suffering.

TRÓCAIRE/COUNCIL FOR JUSTICE AND PEACE

The person grows more, matures more and is sanctified more to the extent that he or she enters into relationships, going out from themselves to live in communion with God, with others and with all creatures.

LAUDATO SI', 240

Prayer for Strength

Every day I need you Lord, but this day especially,
I need some extra strength to face whatever is to come.

This day, more than any other day, I need to feel
you near me … to fortify my courage and to overcome
my fear.

By myself, I cannot meet the challenge of the hour …
How much frail human creatures need a Higher Power
sustaining them in all that life may bring.

And so, dear Lord, hold my trembling hand …
Be with me, Lord, this day, to know your guiding hand
in all, to know your Blessed Presence, ever near.
Amen.

ST JOHN XXIII

Let us ask the Lord to help us understand the law of
love. How good it is to have this law! How much good
it does us to love one another, in spite of everything.
EVANGELII GAUDIUM, 101

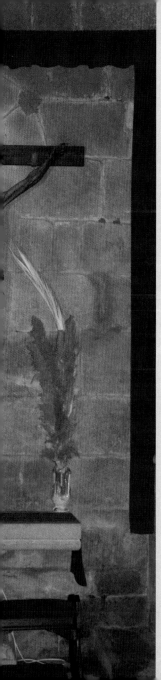

I Keep My Eyes on the Crucified and Risen Lord

Pondering the Passion I am struck by the profound loneliness of the Lord, especially in the Agony, but perhaps all his life in ways …

In writing I hope to carry His peace to those who live with the shadow of death. It is a shadow that I have seen through in these weeks: it loses its sting when I keep my eyes on the Crucified and Risen Lord.

MICHAEL PAUL GALLAGHER

Blessed be the God and Father of our Lord Jesus Christ, the Father of mercies and the God of all consolation, who consoles us in all our affliction, so that we may be able to console those who are in any affliction with the consolation with which we ourselves are consoled by God.

2 CORINTHIANS 1:3–4

To follow Christ the perfect human is to become more human oneself.

GAUDIUM ET SPES, 41

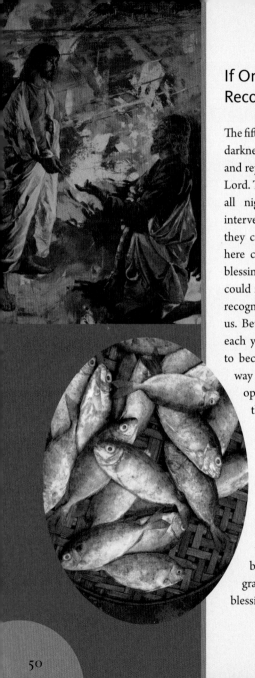

If Only We Could Recognise Him

The fifty days of Easter are a time beyond darkness in which to count our blessings and rejoice in the presence of the Risen Lord. The fishermen had caught nothing all night, but following the Lord's intervention they netted so many fish they could not haul them in. The fish here can represent blessings, so many blessings coming our way if only we could recognise them; if only we could recognise him and the gifts he brings to us. Between Easter Day and Pentecost each year we are given time to reflect, to become aware again in a particular way of the Risen Lord present to us, opening the Scriptures, breaking the bread, passing around the cup of salvation. The message of this season is a message not just for that moment but for all of life. Jesus guides us into New Life, into the fullness of life. Christ's love blesses our lives. In our love for him we open our hearts to all that he gives, to generosity beyond compare, to abundant grace, and recognise the many blessings of life lived in God's love.

GARETH BYRNE

The Joy of Easter

At the end of Lent, at the Chrism Mass, the Bishop blesses the oil of the sick and the oil of catechumens, and consecrates the sacred chrism. These oils are to be used in celebrations of the sacraments; and during the Easter season those oils flow in abundance, at Baptisms and Confirmations. Easter is also an appropriate time for the sacrament of the Anointing of the Sick. The prayer that accompanies the Anointing of the Sick is a Resurrection prayer: 'May the Lord who frees you from sin save you and raise you up' ...

Find ways for the sick and the homebound to share the joy of the Easter season ... Encourage the parish to pray for those who are sick and homebound, and encourage those who are sick and homebound to pray for others as well – the newly baptised, the children of the parish preparing for their first Holy Communion, young people preparing for Confirmation. This is one more way for them to feel part of their parish community even when they cannot be present at Sunday Mass.

For many parishes Easter marks the beginning of the wedding season. Outside the church, the sun is beginning to shine, and flowers and trees are bursting into bloom. Inside, everything speaks of resurrection and new life. It is the perfect time for a wedding.

CORINNA LAUGHLIN *ET AL.*

The Holy Spirit Will Teach You Everything

Jesus said to his disciples, 'I have said these things to you while I am still with you. But the Advocate, the Holy Spirit, whom the Father will send in my name, will teach you everything, and remind you of all I have said to you. Peace I leave with you; my peace I give you.'

JOHN 14:25–7

The Holy Spirit can be said to possess an infinite creativity, proper to the divine mind, which knows how to loosen the knots of human affairs, including the most complex and inscrutable.

ST JOHN PAUL II, *CATECHESIS*, 24 APRIL 1991

Come, Holy Spirit, fill the Church with wisdom and compassion, that she may be a sign and instrument of Christ's love for all people, we pray.

Come, Holy Spirit, and fill the whole world, guiding all nations to reconciliation and lasting peace, we pray.

Come, Holy Spirit, Father of the poor, and bless those burdened by injustice, poverty, hunger, or disease; relieve their suffering and rekindle their hope, we pray.

Come, Holy Spirit, and visit the hearts of all who are experiencing doubt, all who feel burdened by guilt, and all who have grown lukewarm in the practice of their faith; fill them with faith and love, we pray.

CORINNA LAUGHLIN *ET AL.*

Molaigí an Tiarna, Alleluia

Molaigí an Thiarna, an chiníocha go leír, Alleluia.
Molaigí É, a náisiúin uile.
                    Molaigí an Tiarna, Alleluia.

Óir bíonn carthanacht trocaireadh dúinn ag dul i méid i gconaí, Alleluia.
Agus maireann fírinne an Tiarna go deo.
                    Molaigí an Tiarna, Alleluia.
                            KEVIN HEALY, BASED ON PSALM 116

O praise the Lord, all you nations,
acclaim him all you people!

Strong is his love for us;
he is faithful for ever.

                                        PSALM 116

To praise another human being or part of God's creation means to recognise,
to celebrate and to proclaim the goodness which is in them. All goodness
comes from God, and is a sign of his presence in the world he has made.
                                        A.M. ALLCHIN

Meditating on the Mystery of Salvation

The Rosary is a beautiful way of meditating on the mystery of salvation. Pope Saint John Paul II proposed that in addition to the three sets of mysteries established down through the centuries, a fourth set of mysteries be introduced; the Mysteries of Light (or Luminous Mysteries). There was a great tradition in Ireland and elsewhere of the Rosary as a family prayer recited together as the day drew to a close. Any one decade of the Rosary can be prayed on its own, consisting of one Our Father, ten Hail Marys and one Glory Be to the Father. It is most common to pray the five decades of a particular Mystery together, using a set of Rosary beads as a meditative tool to free the mind of counting, and reflecting not so much on the words of the prayers but on the Mystery itself. When praying five decades it is traditional to bless yourself, and begin with the Apostles' Creed, one Our Father, three Hail Marys and a Glory Be to the Father. The Rosary is concluded with the Hail Holy Queen. It is worth reflecting on how the repetition of the prayers associated with the Rosary can be employed as a way of drawing oneself into close prayerful connection with Mary and with her son Jesus.

The Joyful Mysteries (Monday and Saturday)

1. **The Annunciation**
   Mary learns that she has been chosen to be the mother of Jesus

2. **The Visitation**
   Mary visits Elizabeth, who tells her that she will always be remembered

3. **The Nativity**
   Jesus is born in a stable in Bethlehem

4. **The Presentation**
   Mary and Joseph take the infant Jesus to the Temple to present him to God

5. **The Finding of Jesus in the Temple**
   Jesus is found in the Temple discussing his faith with the teachers

The Mysteries of Light (Thursday)

1. **The Baptism of Jesus in the River Jordan**
   God proclaims that Jesus is his beloved Son

2. **The Wedding Feast at Cana**
   At Mary's request, Jesus performs his first miracle

3. **The Proclamation of the Kingdom of God**
   Jesus calls all to conversion and service to the Kingdom

4. **The Transfiguration of Jesus**
   Jesus is revealed in glory to Peter, James, and John

5. **The Institution of the Eucharist**
   Jesus offers his Body and Blood at the Last Supper

The Sorrowful Mysteries (Tuesday and Friday)

1. **The Agony in the Garden**
   Jesus prays in the Garden of Gethsemane on the night before he dies

2. **The Scourging at the Pillar**
   Jesus is lashed with whips

3. **The Crowning With Thorns**
   Jesus is mocked and crowned with thorns

4. **The Carrying of the Cross**
   Jesus carries the cross that will be used to crucify him

5. **The Crucifixion**
   Jesus is nailed to the cross and dies

The Glorious Mysteries (Wednesday and Sunday)

1. **The Resurrection**
   God the Father raises Jesus from the dead

2. **The Ascension**
   Jesus returns to his Father in heaven

3. **The Coming of the Holy Spirit**
   The Holy Spirit comes to bring new life to the disciples

4. **The Assumption of Mary**
   At the end of her life on earth, Mary is taken body and soul into heaven

5. **The Coronation of Mary**
   Mary is crowned as Queen of Heaven and Earth

I Receive Remarkable Letters

I receive remarkable letters. They are opened for me, unfolded and spread out before my eyes, in a daily ritual that gives the arrival of the post the character of a hushed and holy ceremony. I carefully read each letter myself. Some of them are serious in tone, discussing the meaning of life, invoking the supremacy of the soul, the mystery of every existence. And by a curious reversal, the people who focus most closely on the fundamental questions tend to be the people I had known only superficially. Their small talk had masked hidden depths. Had I been blind and deaf, or does it take the glare of disaster to show a person's true nature?

Other letters simply relate the small events that punctuate the passage of time: roses picked at dusk, the laziness of a rainy Sunday, a child crying himself to sleep. Capturing the moment, these small slices of life, these small gusts of happiness, move me more deeply than all the rest. A couple of lines or eight pages, a Middle Eastern stamp or a suburban postmark … I hoard all these letters like treasure. One day I hope to fasten them end to end in a half-mile streamer, to float in the wind like a banner raised to the glory of friendship.

JEAN-DOMINIQUE BAUBY

Memories Make the Past Present

Memories make the past present. When we gather to share the story of Jesus' life, death and Resurrection, we do more than recall a series of past events. In the present moment, we experience here and now the saving presence of Jesus among us and we look forward with hope to the future. As we take part in the Eucharist, the Lord who died and rose again breaks through the limitations and barriers of time and place …

When we remember our loved ones and bring our memory of them and their story into the present moment, we literally re-member them into the community. Remembering echoes their story and significance into our lives again.

JACKIE WILLIAMS

It is always possible to pray. The time of the Christian is that of the risen Christ who is with us always, no matter what tempests may arise. Our time is in the hands of God.

CATECHISM OF THE CATHOLIC CHURCH, 2743

Night Prayer

In your mercy, Lord,
dispel the darkness of this night.
Let your household so sleep in peace,
that at the dawn of a new day,
they may, with joy, waken in your name.
Through Christ our Lord.
Amen.

TUESDAY NIGHT PRAYER

God hears our requests as if they were for his own benefit. The joy he has in giving is more than the joy we have in receiving. So ask freely for what you need; but ask only for what is worthy of his goodness.

St GREGORY NAZIANZEN (c.329–90)

There are few fixed relationships in liquid modernity. A vocation, whether to be a priest or a religious, married or to practise a profession, goes against this grain. It is a witness to our hope that my life as a whole may have some sense. I do not just do things; I am called to be someone, and a vocation is part of saying who I am.

TIMOTHY RADCLIFFE

I First Loved You

God has loved us from all eternity.
So he says: Remember I first loved you.
You had not come to be,
nor did the world exist,
but I loved you already.
From all eternity I have loved you.

ST ALPHONSUS (1696–1787)

In God and with God, I love even the person whom I do not like or even know. This can only take place on the basis of an intimate encounter with God, an encounter that has become a communion of will, even affecting my feelings. Then I learn to look on this other person not simply with my eyes and my feelings, but from the perspective of Jesus Christ. His friend is my friend … Seeing with the eyes of Christ, I can give to others much more than their outward necessities; I can give them the look of love which they crave … No longer is it a question, then, of a 'commandment' imposed from without and calling for the impossible, but rather of a freely bestowed experience of love from within, a love which by its very nature must then be shared with others. Love grows through love. Love is 'divine' because it comes from God and unites us to God.

BENEDICT XVI, *DEUS CARITAS EST*, 18

The Gospel is light, it is newness, it is energy, it is salvation.

BLESSED PAUL VI, *ECCLESIAM SUAM*, 59

Where the Good Way Lies

Thus says the Lord:
Stand at the crossroads, and look,
and ask for the ancient paths, where
the good way lies; and walk in it,
and find rest for your souls.

JEREMIAH 6:16

To let go of anger, wrath, violence and
revenge are necessary conditions to
living joyfully.

FRANCIS, *MISERICORDIAE VULTUS*, 9

The family must be a place where,
when something good happens to
one of its members, they know that
others will be there to celebrate it
with them.

AMORIS LAETITIA, 110

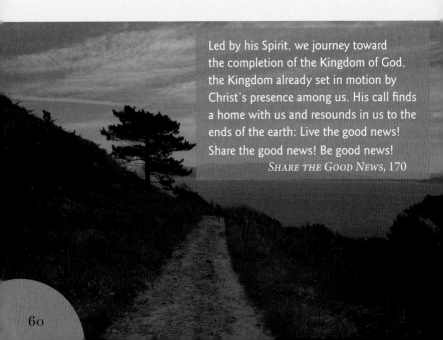

Led by his Spirit, we journey toward
the completion of the Kingdom of God,
the Kingdom already set in motion by
Christ's presence among us. His call finds
a home with us and resounds in us to the
ends of the earth: Live the good news!
Share the good news! Be good news!

SHARE THE GOOD NEWS, 170

A Final Blessing

I leave you now with this prayer:

that the Lord Jesus will reveal Himself to each
   one of you,
that He will give you the strength to go out and
   profess that you are Christian,
that He will show you that He alone can fill your
   hearts.

Accept His freedom and embrace His truth,
and be messengers of the certainty that you have
   been truly liberated
through the death and resurrection of the Lord
   Jesus.

This will be the new experience, the powerful
   experience,
that will generate, through you, a more just
   society and a better world.

God bless you, and may the joy of Jesus be
   always with you. Amen.
                              St John Paul II

Love always gives life.
                    Amoris laetitia, 165

Love never ends.
                    1 Corinthians 13:8a

Acknowledgements

p. 6 Jean Vanier, *Community and Growth*, London: Darton, Longman and Todd, 1979, p. 136.

p. 9 'Fall in Love, Stay in Love', attributed to Fr Pedro Arrupe SJ (1907–1991) from *Finding God in All Things: A Marquette Prayer Book*, Milwaukee, WI: Marquette University, 2009. Used by permission.

p. 10 'Ever the Maker and Keeper of My Days', based on Ps 139. Words and music: Bernadette Farrell, © Bernadette Farrell, 1992. Published in Portland, OR: OCP Publications.

p. 11 Daniel A. Helminiak, *Spiritual Development: An Interdisciplinary Study*, Chicago: Loyola University Press, 1987, pp. 10–11.

p. 18 Daniel O'Leary, *New Hearts for New Models*, Dublin: Columba Press, 1997, p. 110.

p. 18 United States Conference of Catholic Bishops, 'Prayer for Vocations: Prayer 34', *United States Conference of Catholic Bishops* [website], http://www.usccb.org/prayer-and-worship/prayers-and-devotions/prayers/prayers-for-vocations.cfm, accessed 30 September 2016.

p. 20 Meg Bateman, 'Lightness', translated from the Gaelic by the author in Neil Astley (ed.), *Staying Alive: Real Poems for Unreal Times*, Northumberland: Bloodaxe Books, 2002, p. 293.

p. 21 Peter G. van Breemen, *Called by Name*, Denville, NJ: Dimension Books, 1976, pp. 234–5.

p. 22 Henri J.M. Nouwen, *The Road to Daybreak: A Spiritual Journey*, New York: Doubleday, 1988.

p. 28 Marsha Sinetar, *Spiritual Intelligence: What We Can Learn from the Early Awakening Child*, New York: Orbis Books, 2000, p. 1.

p. 28 Anne Frank, *The Diary of a Young Girl*, New York: Bantam Books, 1993, p. 171.

p. 29 Stuart Hample and Eric Marshall, *Children's Letters to God*, New York: Workman Publishing, 2009.

p. 30 Prayer is reproduced with permission from *The Book of Saints*, by Victor Hoagland CP © 2014 by Catholic Book Publishing Corp., NJ. All rights reserved. www.catholicbookpublishing.com

p. 34 Celtic Rune of Hospitality, trans. Seán Ó Duinn, quoted in John J. O'Riordain, *The Music of What Happens: Celtic Spirituality – A View from the Inside*, Dublin: Columba Press, 1997, p. 67.

p. 35 Timothy O'Grady and Steve Pyke, *I Could Read the Sky*, London: The Harvill Press, 1998, p. 146.

p. 35 Siegfried Sassoon, 'Everyone Sang', *Picture Show*, London: Heinemann, 1920. Copyright Siegfried Sassoon by kind permission of the Estate of George Sassoon.

p. 37 'Suscipe of Catherine McAuley', words adapted and music by Elaine Deasy RSM, found on Mercy International Association's *Circle of Mercy* CD, © Elaine Deasy RSM. Original translation of 'Suscipe of Catherine McAuley' by Sister Dolores Neratka. Used with permission.

p. 38 Dermot O'Brien, *Small World: Haiku on the Way*, Dublin: Veritas, 2004, pp. 56, 15, 42.

p. 38 Donal Neary, *Masses with Young People*, Dublin: Columba Press, 1985, pp. 18–19. Used with permission.

p. 41 St Teresa of Calcutta, 'Help Us to Spread Your Fragrance'.

p. 42 Donal Harrington, *Tomorrow's Parish: A Vision and a Path*, Dublin: Columba Press, 2015, pp. 118–19.

p. 44 Michael Downey, 'Disability, the Disabled' in Michael Downey (ed.), *The New Dictionary of Catholic Spirituality*, Collegeville, MN: The Liturgical Press, 1993, p. 274.

p. 45 Jean Vanier, *Community and Growth*, London: Darton, Longman and Todd, 1979, pp. 94–5.

p. 45 Philip North and John North (eds), *Sacred Space: House of God, Gate of Heaven*, London: Continuum, 2007, p. 129.

p. 46, p. 49 Michael Paul Gallagher, *Into Extra Time: Living Through the Final Stages of Cancer and Jottings Along the Way*, Dublin: Messenger Publications, 2016, p. 110.

p. 46 Jean-Pierre de Caussade, *The Sacrament of the Present Moment*, tr. Kitty Muggeridge, London: Fount Paperbacks, 1989, p. 125.

p. 47 Trócaire/Council for Justice and Peace, 'From Reflection to Action: Catholic Social Teaching and the Work of Justice and Peace', Irish Episcopal Conference: Maynooth, 2016, p. 11.

p. 51, p. 52 Corinna Laughlin et al., *2011 Sourcebook for Sundays, Seasons, and Weekdays*, Chicago: Liturgy Training Publications, pp. 184, 218.

p. 53 A.M. Allchin, *Praise Above All: Discovering the Welsh Tradition*, Cardiff: University of Wales Press, 1991, p. 6.

p. 53 Kevin Healy OSB, 'Molaigí an Tiarna, Alleluia', *Alleluia! Amen!* Margaret Daly (ed.), Dublin: Veritas, 1978, p. 50.

p. 56 Jean-Dominique Bauby, *The Diving-Bell and the Butterfly*, London/New York/Toronto/Sydney: Harper Perennial, 2008, pp. 91.

p. 57 Jackie Williams, 'Like Mary, in Grief', *The Tablet*, 6 February 2016, p. 14.

p. 58 Timothy Radcliffe, *What is the Point of Being a Christian?*, London: Burns & Oates, 2005, p. 198.

p. 61 St John Paul II, 'A Final Blessing', *Go in Peace: A Gift of Enduring Love*, Joseph Durepos (ed.), Chicago: Loyola Press, 2003, p. 221. Used with permission.

Cover image: St Mary's Church, Killymard, Co. Donegal.

All photographs © Gareth Byrne.

Love One Another As I Have Loved You is a book of prayers, meditations and reflections compiled by Gareth Byrne in response to the publication of *Amoris laetitia*, Pope Francis' apostolic exhortation 'on Love in the Family'. This collection includes reflective pieces on family, friendship and community and invites readers to take time in the healing presence of Jesus, opening themselves to the Spirit of God's love at work in their lives and in their relationships.

With the World Meeting of Families to be hosted in Ireland, by the Archdiocese of Dublin, in August 2018, we look to the future inspired by the joyful humanity and commitment of Pope Francis who reminds us of God's unconditional love for us revealed in Jesus. Conscious that we are less than perfect, we open ourselves to being renewed by Christ's love and the love we have for one another.

> 'Love does not have to be perfect for us to value it. The other person loves me as best they can, with all their limits, but the fact that love is imperfect does not mean that it is untrue or unreal. It is real, albeit limited and earthly.'
>
> *Amoris laetitia*, 113

Gareth Byrne is a priest of the Archdiocese of Dublin and chairman of the Dublin Diocesan Council of Priests. Dr Byrne is the Director of the 'Mater Dei Centre for Catholic Education', DCU Institute of Education, Dublin City University.

www.worldmeeting2018.ie

VERITAS
www.veritas.ie

PRINTED IN IRELAND
978 1 84730 760 6
www.veritas.ie